THE MYSTERY OF
UFOs

Chris Oxlade

Heinemann
LIBRARY

www.heinemann.co.uk/library
Visit our website to find out more information about Heinemann Library books.

To order:
 Phone 44 (0) 1865 888112
Send a fax to 44 (0) 1865 314091
 Visit the Heinemann Bookshop at www.heinemann.co.uk/library to browse our
catalogue and order online.

First published in Great Britain by Heinemann Library, Halley Court, Jordan Hill, Oxford OX2 8EJ, part of Harcourt Education. Heinemann is a registered trademark of Harcourt Education Ltd.

Editorial: Clare Lewis
Design: Victoria Bevan and Q2A
Production: Helen McCreath

Printed in China

10 digit ISBN 0 431 01888 X
13 digit ISBN 978 0 431 01888 1
10 09 08 07 06
10 9 8 7 6 5 4 3 2 1

British Library Cataloguing in Publication Data
Oxlade, Chris
Can Science Solve: The Mystery of UFOs – 2nd edition
001.9'42
A full catalogue record for this book is available from the British Library.

Acknowledgements
The publishers would like to thank the following for permission to reproduce photographs:
Aviation Picture Library: p19; Mary Evans Picture Library: pp13 (upper), 24, 26, K Aarsleff p17, G Adamski p10, C Hart Jnr p9; Fortean Picture Library: pp6, 7, W Akins p28, B Askew p20, D Stacy p13 (Lower), F Taylor p23, A Vieira p29, P Villa p4; Science Photo Library: NASA p15, D Parker p18.

Cover picture of a flying saucer, reproduced with permission of Corbis/Roger Ball.

The publishers would like to thank Sarah Williams for her assistance in the preparation of this book.

Every effort has been made to contact copyright holders of any material reproduced in this book. Any omissions will be rectified in subsequent printings if notice is given to the publishers.

The paper used to print this book comes from sustainable resources.

CONTENTS

UNSOLVED MYSTERIES

For hundreds of years, people have been interested in and puzzled by mysterious places, creatures and events. Is there really a monster living in Loch Ness? Did the lost city of Atlantis ever exist? Are crop circles clever hoaxes or alien messages? Are UFOs tricks of the light, or actually vehicles from outer space? Some of these mysteries have baffled scientists, who have spent years trying to find the answer. But just how far can science go? Can it really explain the seemingly unexplainable? Are there some mysteries which science simply cannot solve? Read on, and make your own mind up...

This book tells you about the history of UFOs, retells eyewitness accounts, and looks at the different theories which attempt to explain them.

What is a UFO?

As you probably know, the letters UFO stand for Unidentified Flying Object. Most people think that UFO is just another way of saying 'alien spaceship', but it is not. A UFO is any light or object in the sky which cannot be explained. Some UFOs are not actually seen by the human eye, but are detected by **radar,** such as the radars used by air traffic controllers.

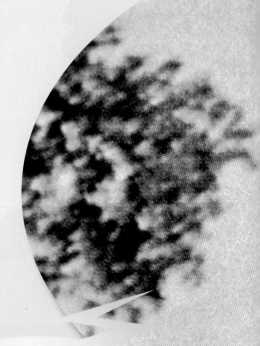

A photograph of a UFO taken by Paul Villa near Albuquerque, New Mexico, USA.

It is important to remember that more than 90 per cent of reported UFOs become IFOs – Identified Flying Objects. They might be aircraft, planets or weather balloons, for example, but this still leaves many real UFOs. What are they? The most romantic theory is that UFOs are alien spacecraft spying on the Earth. Some scientists believe that all UFOs are actually natural objects in the atmosphere, such as clouds. Others believe that they are **hallucinations** or hoaxes.

Most serious scientists dismiss UFOs as nonsense made up by cranks. This is perhaps not surprising considering the wild and unbelievable stories of alien **abductions** in UFOs that so often appear in newspapers and television programmes. But is there anything science can do to help solve the mystery?

BEGINNINGS OF A MYSTERY

The UFO **phenomenon** first became international news in the late 1940s, but there are many reports of strange objects in the sky from well before that – even from thousands of years earlier. Some UFOlogists (people that study UFOs) think that the Star of Bethlehem, which was said to have appeared at the time of the birth of Jesus Christ, was a UFO. How else, they say, would it be able to move and stop, and indicate the exact building where Jesus was born?

Some UFOlogists believe this 8000-year-old painting from the Sahara Desert is of an alien space traveller.

Early UFOs

One of the earliest UFO sightings was made in China in 1914 BC, where 'ten flying suns' caused panic among the people. In 216 BC, Roman troops saw several 'ships in the sky' over Italy. There are several reports from Japan: in AD 1180 there was a 'glowing vessel' in the sky; in 1235 there were strange moving lights overhead; and in 1749 thousands of Japanese people saw three huge flying objects for four days.

UFO hotspots

There have been reports of UFOs from all over the world, but there tend to be more reports from some areas than others. Where are these UFO 'hotspots'? Most tend to be in densely populated areas in countries where people are interested in UFOs, so more reports would be expected because there are more people looking for UFOs in the sky. Top hotspots include Mexico City, Warminster in England and Gulf Breeze in Florida.

In 1897, a farmer in Kansas, USA, saw a 'huge, cigar-shaped object the length of a football field' descend from the sky into one of his fields. Inside the craft's glass cabin were six of the 'strangest beings ever seen'. The ship rose again, carrying away a cow on the end of a rope.

During World War II, pilots from both sides who flew over Europe occasionally saw small balls of light which seemed to follow their aircraft. The 'foo fighters' (perhaps after the French word for fire – feu), have never been explained.

DID YOU SEE THAT?

Here are some of the most famous UFO sightings of recent times. There are more sightings and stories on page 10.

Kenneth Arnold, Mount Rainier, USA, 1947

Kenneth Arnold was flying over a mountain range searching for the wreck of a military transport plane when he saw a flash of light. Looking in the direction of the flash, he saw nine objects moving 'like a saucer would if you skipped it across water'. He estimated that they were about 20 metres across and were flying at more than 2000 kilometres per hour – three times faster than any aircraft of the time could manage. Arnold's is one of the most famous sightings of all because the press took Arnold's description and coined the phrase 'flying saucer'. Within days of its appearance in the newspapers, there were a huge number of UFO reports from all over the USA.

Classes of encounter

American UFOlogist Dr J Allen Hynek devised this classification for encounters with UFOs and aliens:

- CE1 (Close Encounter of the First Kind): When a UFO is spotted at a distance, such as a light or object in the sky.

- CE2: When a UFO leaves a sign of its presence, such as marks on the ground.

- CE3: When the eyewitness sees alien creatures inside or outside a UFO.

- CE4: When a person is abducted by aliens.

- CE5: When a person talks or communicates with an alien.

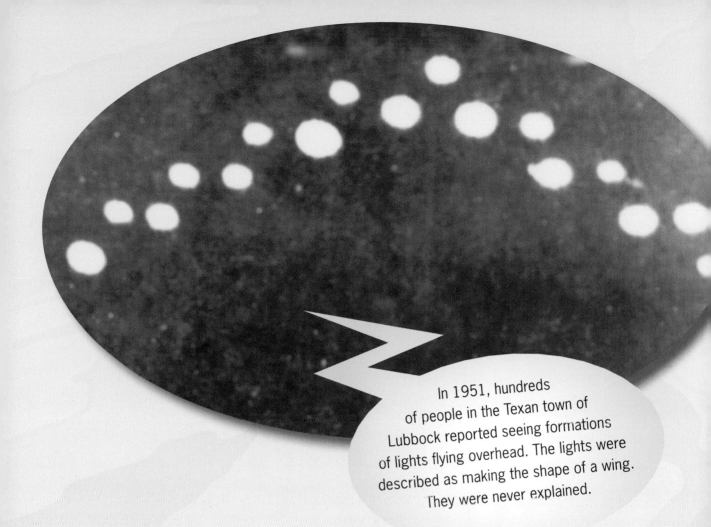

In 1951, hundreds of people in the Texan town of Lubbock reported seeing formations of lights flying overhead. The lights were described as making the shape of a wing. They were never explained.

UFO on film, New Zealand, 1978

An Australian TV reporter and a film crew were on a plane looking for a UFO that had been spotted a few days earlier. They saw, and filmed, several bright lights in the sky and an object with a bright base and dome which kept track with the plane. **Radar** on the ground confirmed that an object was there, but the sighting was never explained.

The Trident sighting, Portugal, 1976

A British Airways Trident aircraft was south of Lisbon when the crew heard air traffic control reports of a UFO on their radar. Out of the windows, the crew and passengers of the Trident saw a bright light and a long cigar-shaped object approaching the light. The crews of two other aircraft confirmed the sighting. An hour later, on the Trident's return flight, the crew detected by radar an object the size of a supertanker in the same place, but saw nothing.

MEETING THE ALIENS

On these pages you can read reports of UFOs which include meetings with aliens and **abductions** by aliens. Mostly, the people who claim to have been abducted find it hard to remember what has happened to them. All they know is that several hours are missing from their memories and that something odd has happened. Hypnosis can often help them to remember.

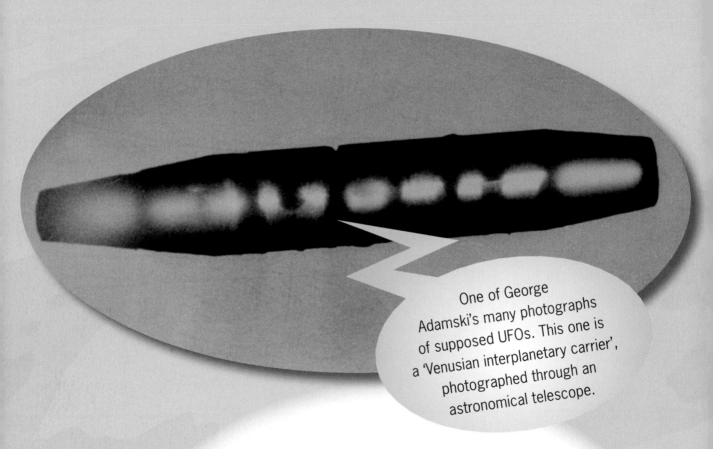

One of George Adamski's many photographs of supposed UFOs. This one is a 'Venusian interplanetary carrier', photographed through an astronomical telescope.

All in the mind?

Psychologists suggest that alien abductions are not real events. They believe that people who claim they have been abducted have just imagined it all while they are in a dream-like state, which the psychologists call sleep paralysis. This can also happen just before you fall properly asleep, and it can make you feel awake while you dream.

George Adamski, California, 1952

This celebrated case is the first example of a human meeting an alien. Adamski claims that on one afternoon in 1952, while he was watching and photographing a flying saucer, a human-like alien approached him. Using hand gestures and telepathy, the alien told Adamski that he was from Venus. The incident was witnessed from a distance by two families. This meeting was the first of many – Adamski claims to have been taken by flying saucer on trips to Mars, Saturn and Jupiter, where he met inhabitants of each planet. Adamski has no proof of his encounters.

Betty and Barney Hill, New Hampshire, 1961

This was the first widely-reported case of people being abducted by aliens. The Hills were driving home late at night when they saw a bright light ahead. The light got brighter and closer and appeared to be moving. Eventually they stopped the car and Barney got out and approached the object, which was hovering above the ground. Seeing a dozen 'people' inside, he fled back to the car. The couple drove off, but were in a 'sedated' state for some time. Ten days later, Betty began to have nightmares in which aliens took them from their car and examined them in a spaceship. She became convinced that she was remembering real events. Under hypnosis, both Betty and Barney recalled the abduction, but nothing can be proved.

IT'S OFFICIAL

Today, the world's governments tend to take little interest in UFO reports from the public, but the military do investigate UFOs that their **radars** detect. In the past, however, they took reports more seriously. In the USA in the 1940s, '50s and '60s, the Air Force was responsible for investigating UFOs. At the time, the **Cold War** was at its height, and the American people were concerned about an attack from the Soviet Union. Some UFOs were thought to be bizarre new Soviet aircraft. The Air Force attempted to explain UFOs without admitting that they could not account for some sightings.

Project Blue Book

Between 1952 and 1969, the United States Air Force (USAF) kept a record of all UFO reports it received. This record was called Project Blue Book. In all, it listed 12,318 sightings. All were investigated and most were explained, except for 701 sightings which remained a mystery.

Men in black

You may have heard of the 1998 film 'Men in Black', but do you know what men in black were? They were men in dark suits and dark glasses who visited UFO eyewitnesses and investigators and threatened them to keep quiet about their experiences. Some people claim that they were agents of the US government; others that they were aliens themselves!

The conspiracy theory

Many UFOlogists are convinced that the governments of the world, especially the US government, have conclusive evidence that some UFOs are actually alien spacecraft. They claim that there is a cover-up, mainly by the CIA (the US government-run Central Intelligence Agency), to prevent panic. In the USA, a group of engineers and scientists called the Condon Committee was set up by the US Air Force to investigate unsolved UFOs. They concluded that none were alien spacecraft – a conclusion derided by UFOlogists.

This debris, found in 1947 near Roswell Air Force Base, New Mexico, is claimed to be the remains of either a weather balloon (by the US Air Force) or a flying saucer (by many UFOlogists).

There are also alleged reports that several astronauts have encountered UFOs, including one that Neil Armstrong saw a fleet of huge spacecraft on the Moon during the *Apollo 11* trip in 1969. The **conspiracy theorists** say that the astronauts were told to keep quiet and that the published photographs of the Moon landings were faked by **NASA** in a film studio in order to cover up this fact.

Many strange lights have been seen in a military area nicknamed 'Area 51' by UFOlogists. The official story is that the area does not exist.

ARE WE ALONE?

The case for UFOs being alien spacecraft would seem more believable if we could find evidence that there was actually intelligent life in other parts of the Universe. So how likely is other life, and how could we find out if it was there?

The chances of life

We know that the Earth is the only planet in our **Solar System** where there is life. The chances of intelligent life evolving on the Earth must have been very small indeed, but it happened.

Astronomers know that there are thousands of millions of stars like our Sun in our **galaxy,** and there are thousands of millions more galaxies in the Universe. They have found evidence of large planets **orbiting** our neighbouring stars (the stars wobble slightly as the planets move around them), although they have never seen them. If this is the case, it is not unreasonable to think that there may be many Earth-like planets out there where life may have evolved too.

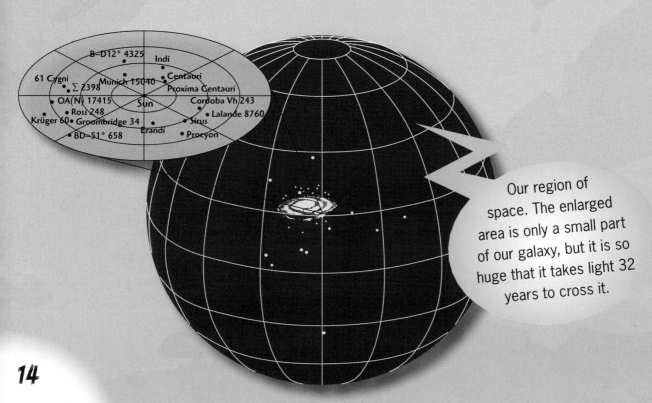

Our region of space. The enlarged area is only a small part of our galaxy, but it is so huge that it takes light 32 years to cross it.

Signals from Earth

Trying to contact life on other planets has one huge problem – the distances involved. Radio signals travel at the speed of light (300,000 kilometres per second), but they still take more than four years to reach even our nearest star neighbour. And then you have to wait for the reply to come back at the same speed. Many of the radio signals we use on Earth for communications are spreading into space, and may be detected by other beings. In 1973 a simple **binary** radio message was sent towards a cluster of stars called M13, in the hope that there is life around one of the many stars there. It will take 25,000 years to reach the cluster.

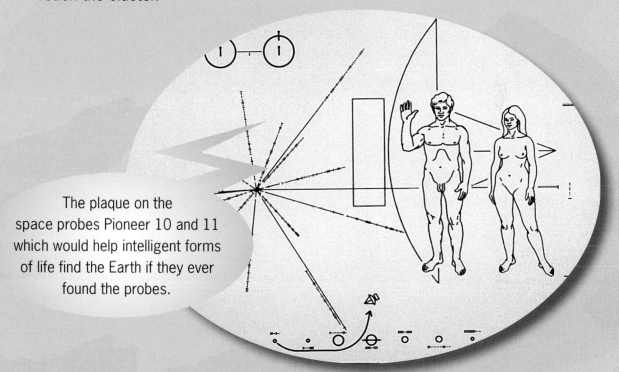

The plaque on the space probes Pioneer 10 and 11 which would help intelligent forms of life find the Earth if they ever found the probes.

Listening out

In 1982, a group of Russian and American scientists set up a project known as SETI (Search for **Extra-Terrestrial** Intelligence) to look for radio signals coming from outer space using a radio telescope. They have listened to thousands of stars without finding anything, but there are millions more to go.

In 1977, American astronomer Bob Dixon detected a 37-second-long powerful radio signal from the area of the **constellation** Sagittarius. But the signal was random and has never been repeated.

TRAVEL TO THE STARS

If we assume that there is other intelligent life in the Universe, could we ever visit it? More importantly for the explanation of UFOs, could members of that intelligent life build a spacecraft and visit us?

The age of civilization

Astronomers think that our **Solar System** was formed about 4500 million years ago. The oldest **fossils** ever found are of simple sea-living organisms 3000 million years old. Creatures began to inhabit the land about 500 million years ago and human-like creatures evolved about 4 million years ago. Farming began about 10,000 years ago, and industry began about 300 years ago. Computers have been developed in the last 40 years. From this, you can see that the pace of technological change is getting faster and faster. As the 21st century starts, our knowledge of science seems vast, but it may be the tip of the iceberg.

Gods or aliens?

There are theories that aliens visited the Earth in ancient times and communicated with people, teaching them technologies way ahead of the time. The main pieces of evidence for this theory are archaeological finds called out-of-place artefacts (OOPARTS) – objects which are thousands of years old but which have modern technologies in them. One example is a 1800-year-old ceramic pot found in Iraq which acts as a battery. Another is a 14-centimetre long glider made in 200 BC which flies perfectly.

Now imagine a planet in another Solar System where things are a million years ahead of us. What sort of scientific knowledge and technology would they have? Would it be advanced enough to build a spacecraft capable of crossing the vast expanse of space between their world and ours? At the speed that our current spacecraft travel (about 40,000 kilometres per hour), it would take about 27,000 years to cover the 4 light years to our nearest star, but with a spacecraft capable of one quarter the speed of light (about 250 million kilometres per hour), it would take about 16 years – much more practical.

These lines in Peru are claimed to be landing areas for UFOs which visited Earth thousands of years ago.

IDENTIFIED OBJECTS

Most of the UFOs reported by the public can actually be put down to perfectly normal objects or **optical illusions** created by the weather. On these pages you can find out which objects are often mistaken for UFOs. On pages 20–23 you can find out about tricks of the weather.

Real flying objects

Aircraft are often reported as UFOs, especially at night when only their lights are visible. Helicopter lights confuse people because helicopters can hover still in the air and move in all directions. Other UFO-like objects are hot-air balloons, airships, weather balloons, kites and birds. Weather balloons are very confusing because they rise very high into the atmosphere and are often silver-coloured, reflecting the sunlight. These shapes are sometimes also distorted by **mirages** (see page 21).

A type of weather balloon called a 'meduse'. You can see how it could be reported as a flying saucer.

Some UFOs are seen on **radar** screens rather than with the naked eye. But radars can be fooled as well as people. Thick clouds, flocks of birds and places where hot and cold air meet can give false radar reflections which look like large objects on a screen.

In the USA, some reports of bizarre shapes in the sky have been explained as experimental aircraft, such as this 'stealth' fighter.

Space objects

Some UFOs are actually in space, but they are objects that **astronomers** know all about. They can be mistaken for strange lights in the sky because they reflect sunlight brightly. For example, the planet Venus, which is the brightest planet in the sky, is often visible in the evening or morning. **Satellites** in low **orbits** around the Earth look like tiny, fast-moving lights when the Sun shines on them. Rockets taking off have also been mistaken for UFOs. Objects which hurtle into the Earth's atmosphere, such as **meteors** and bits of old rockets, burn up, causing a streak of light.

WEIRD WEATHER

It is thought that natural events in the Earth's atmosphere can explain more than 90 per cent of the sightings of strange lights and shapes in the sky. In fact, many UFO researchers are beginning to ignore 'lights in the sky' reports because they are almost certainly atmospheric **phenomena**.

Cloud shapes

How many times have you seen clouds which look like people's faces or animals? Clouds can also be mistaken for classic flying saucers, especially a type called lenticular clouds. These are formed when wind blows over mountain tops and is made to flow up and down like a wave. As the air rises, saucer-shaped clouds are formed.

Stranger still are noctilucent clouds. These are very high-**altitude** clouds, formed up to 80 kilometres up (ten times higher than normal clouds), and made up of ice particles. After sunset, the Sun's rays light up the clouds, making them look like glowing purple spaceships.

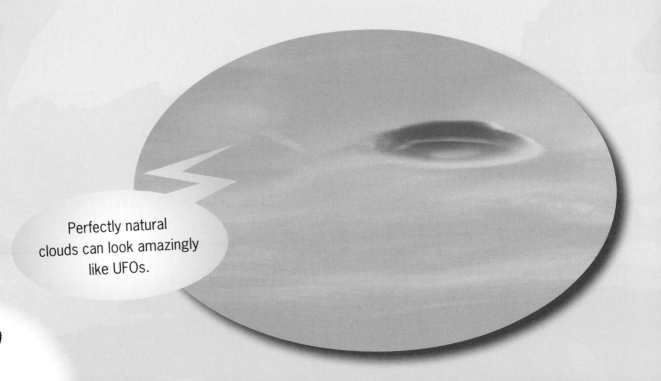

Perfectly natural clouds can look amazingly like UFOs.

Mirages

A **mirage** is an image in the sky of an object which is not really there. People have even seen cities on the opposite side of seas appear in the sky because of mirages. Mirages are caused by changes in the temperature in different layers of air. Light rays coming from objects can be bent up or down as they pass through the layers of air. You might have seen 'puddles' on roads on hot summer days. What you are actually seeing is a mirage of the sky.

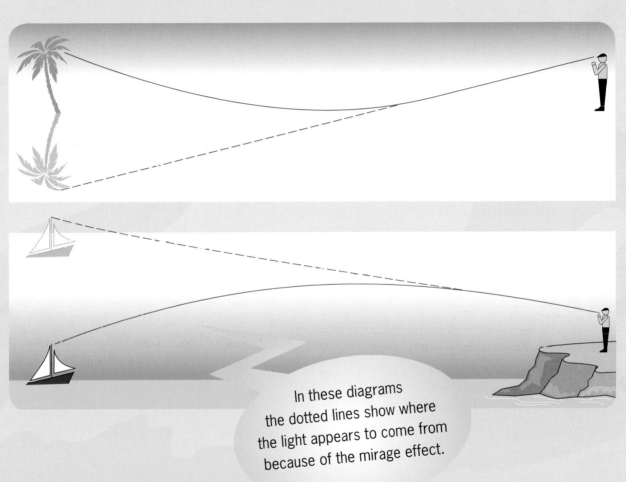

In these diagrams the dotted lines show where the light appears to come from because of the mirage effect.

Sun and Moon dogs

In certain atmospheric conditions, rays of light from the Sun or Moon which would normally pass you by are bent inside clouds. This has the effect of making two more Suns or Moons appear at each side of the real one, looking like hovering lights in the sky. These **optical illusions** are called Sun or Moon dogs.

LIGHTS OR LIGHTNING?

Lightning is the cause of many reports of 'spaceship lights' in the sky. Lightning is caused by **static electricity** that builds up in clouds jumping to the ground. A huge electric current passes through the air, creating a spark-like glow. Sheet lightning (when the whole sky seems to light up) is sometimes thought to be the flash of spaceship engines.

Balls of light and fireballs

One of the strangest and spookiest of all weather **phenomena** is called ball lightning. It normally happens just after a thunderstorm, and looks like a glowing ball of light the size of a football or smaller. Eyewitnesses have seen ball lightning under apparently intelligent control – floating through their houses, following their cars, drifting through their aircraft and even shooting up into the air. It is no wonder that people link ball lightning with spacecraft and aliens. Scientists do not yet understand how ball lightning forms or travels, but they do know that it is an electrical phenomenon because engineers working on electricity power lines have occasionally seen ball lightning form during their work.

Meteor showers

In November 2005 there were numerous sightings of fireballs in the sky over Germany. They led to several reports of UFO sightings. However, scientists believe that the fireballs were caused by a **meteor** shower. A meteor shower is seen when small rocks from space burn up on contact with the Earth's atmosphere.

Glowing vortices

British tornado and whirlwind expert Dr Terence Meaden believes that many UFO reports are linked to another mystery – the formation of crop circles, circular patterns that mysteriously appear in fields of crops. His 'plasma vortex theory' suggests that spinning, glowing bodies of electrically charged air create crop circles, but also look like glowing spacecraft in the sky. They move in a similar 'intelligent' way to ball lightning, and also create humming sounds.

Many believe that crop circles are messages left by aliens. Dr Terence Meaden believes that both phenomena can be explained with his 'plasma vortex theory'.

FAMOUS FAKES

As for all mysterious happenings, there are plenty of UFO hoaxes. They do not help the cause of the people who believe that UFOs are alien spacecraft. They come in two categories: hoax reports of sightings and **abductions**, and fake photographs. Of course, many reports of alien abductions are probably not real, but are dreams that people think are true rather than deliberate fakes.

Group of UFOs, Sheffield, 1962

In 1962, two schoolboys from Sheffield, England, claimed that they had a photograph of a formation of five UFOs flying over Sheffield. The newspapers printed it, calling it the 'best UFO photograph ever', and UFOlogists exhibited it as proof of an alien visit. Several more UFO sightings were reported soon after. Ten years later, one of the boys admitted that the photograph was a fake. They had painted five saucer shapes on a sheet of glass and taken a photograph through it! Amazingly, UFO supporters were reluctant to believe that the photograph was a hoax.

A photograph claimed to have been taken in 1962 of UFOs over Sheffield, England. It is a fake.

The famous Mexico City photograph, suspected to be an elaborate fake.

Fake aliens

There are not only fake photographs of UFOs, but also of aliens which are claimed to have come from spacecraft which have crashed to Earth. One of the most famous is of an alien which is supposed to have survived a crash near Mexico City in the 1950s. It is highly likely to be a fake because the photograph is fuzzy, and no trace has been found of the alien's body or its spacecraft.

Spotting the fake

Some UFO photographs are obvious fakes, but some are more difficult to spot. Photographic experts are normally able to tell whether a photograph has been 'doctored' after it has been taken by looking at the film's grain under a microscope. Two things to look for in a fake photograph are the difference in detail between the landscape and the UFO, and whether the UFO is blurred – this often suggests it is a model. Modern **digital photography** and computer photo-editing will make fakes easier to do and more difficult to spot.

WHY FAKE UFOS?

There are certainly many made-up stories of UFOs and plenty of fake photos of alien spacecraft. But what is the point of making up stories and faking photographs? The Sheffield schoolboys and the hoaxers of the Mexico City photograph probably did it just for fun or to impress their friends. The obvious reason is to try to make some money.

Selling your story

Is there any money to be made out of hoaxing UFOs? Probably – by selling a convincing story to a national newspaper. Certain newspapers would be delighted to have an 'exclusive' alien story. This might have worked in the 1950s, but today, it has to be very convincing and original because of the thousands of reports of UFOs and alien **abductions** which happen every year. Perhaps a good photo of a flying saucer or alien creature would do the trick? Again, it would have to be very good because of the number of cheat photographs created using **digital photography** and computer graphics. However, there are some UFOlogists who have done well by publishing their thoughts in books.

A good hoax could get you into print – in this case in the American magazine Fate.

DONALD KEYHOE—HOW THE SAUCERS FLY

November 1954   35¢

FATE
ANC
MAGAZINE

BOAC's
FLYING
JELLYFISH

AIR CHIEF MARSHAL
LORD DOWDING

"WHY I BELIEVE
IN SAUCERS"

Is it all a hoax?

Some people claim that all stories of little green men are made up and that all photographs of alien spacecraft (not necessarily photographs of lights in the sky) and their occupants are fakes. This may well be true, but it is hard to believe that all UFO reports are made up, especially when many come from apparently reliable witnesses.

How to fake a UFO picture

You could have a go at faking your own flying saucer photograph. Try throwing saucer-shaped objects into the air in front of the camera, taking photographs through a window In which there is a reflection of a light, or through a window with spaceshIps stuck on to it. Or you could try scanning and combining photographs on a computer.

Creating UFO pictures is easy with a computer. People are now difficult to convince as they are used to seeing composite pictures like this in adverts.

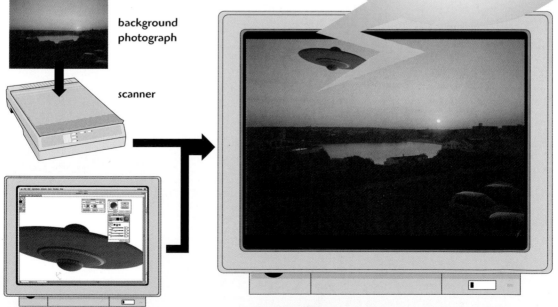

background photograph

scanner

Flying saucer created using 3D computer package.

The two images combined using a graphics package.

WHAT DO YOU THINK?

So, can science really solve the mystery of UFOs? It's certain that science, especially **meteorology**, can explain many UFO reports. In the future, when we understand more about electrical effects in the atmosphere, such as ball lightning, it may be possible to explain many more. But, at the moment, there are still many UFOs that science can't explain.

Are we being visited by intelligent life from other planets?

Sounds convincing...
- Many of the eyewitness reports of sophisticated UFOs come from reliable witnesses such as pilots and military personnel

- There are billions of other planets in the Universe. It seems unlikely that Earth is the only one where intelligent life has evolved

- Although humans have not yet found a way to travel fast enough to visit other planets, life on other planets could be much more technologically advanced than Earth.

But what about...?
- Scientists' attempts to contact life on other planets have not been successful, so far

- If aliens are visiting us, why have they not made themselves known to all of us?

A UFO over the town of Charlotte, South Carolina, USA in 1971.

Aliens about to invade or a flash of lightning? A UFO over Sao Paulo, Brazil in 1984.

There is no doubt that there are UFOs – objects in the sky that we cannot identify. But are they from other planets? With the help of science we are beginning to find other planets in the Universe, but at the moment we don't have the technology to reach them and find out for certain.

What about the other theories? Do you think any of them might be true? Look at the list of theories below and think about the pros and cons of each. Decide which you think are the most convincing.

- Most UFOs are normal, explainable objects such as helicopters or weather balloons

- UFOs are objects in space, such as nearby planets, that reflect the Sun's light brightly

- Clouds and other weather conditions, such as ball lightning, can explain many UFOs

- Governments and the military can explain many UFOs but choose not to, possibly because they are experimental technology.

- All UFO sightings are fakes or **hallucinations**.

What are your conclusions? Are there theories you can dismiss without further investigation? Do you have any theories of your own? Try to keep an open mind. Remember that science is constantly evolving and new discoveries are being made all the time. Just because something can't be proved scientifically now, doesn't mean this will always be the case.

GLOSSARY

abduction kidnapping

altitude the height of an object above the Earth's surface, normally measured in metres or feet

astronomer a person who studies space and the objects in space

binary a simple code made up of the digits 1 and 0, or on and off signals

Cold War the period which began after World War II and lasted into the 1960s, when there was a political struggle between the USA and countries of Western Europe on one side and the countries of Eastern Europe, headed by the Soviet Union, on the other side

conspiracy theory a theory that says that a group of people have plotted together to keep information from the public

constellation a group of stars which seem to form a pattern when they are seen from the Earth

digital photography photography using a camera which stores photographs as numbers inside memory chips instead of on film. The photographs can easily be copied on to a computer and edited on screen.

extra-terrestrial describes any object or being which does not come from the Earth

fossil the remains of an ancient animal or plant (normally a prehistoric one) which has been buried under the ground and has gradually turned to rock

galaxy an enormous cloud of stars in space, which can contain billions of stars. Our own galaxy is called the Milky Way.

hallucination when you think you see or hear something which is not really there

meteor a piece of rock, dust or ice from space which hurtles into the Earth's atmosphere, where friction with the air makes it glow white hot. It makes a streak of light across the sky.

meteorology the study of the Earth's atmosphere and what causes the weather

mirage an optical illusion which makes objects appear in mid air. Mirages are caused by light being bent through layers of warm air near the ground on hot days.

NASA (National Aeronautics and Space Administration) the organization in the USA that controls the US space programme

optical illusion an image seen by the eye which is not what is seems. For example, a flick book shows a series of still pictures which appear to be a moving image when seen in quick succession.

orbit the path that an object, such as a moon or a satellite, takes as it moves around a star or a planet

phenomenon a remarkable or unexplained happening

radar a device which can detect objects in the air. It sends out radio waves and detects any which return because they bounce off objects. It shows the objects on a screen.

satellite an object which moves around a star, planet or moon in an orbit

Solar System the Sun and its family of planets and moons

static electricity the electricity which builds up on objects which are rubbed together. For example, your clothes build up static electricity when they rub together, which makes them attract dust and hair.

Find out more

You can find out more about UFOs in books and on the Internet. Use a search engine such as www.yahooligans.com to search for information. A search for "UFO" will bring back lots of results, but it may be difficult to find the information you want. Try refining your search to look for some of the people and ideas mentioned in this book, such as "George Adamski" or "SETI".

More Books to Read

Eyewitness Readers: Invaders from Outer Space: Real-Life Stories of UFOs, Philip Brooks and Tony Smith (Dorling Kindersley, 1999)

Forensic Files: Investigating UFOs, Paul Mason (Heinemann Library, 2004)

Out There? Mysterious Encounters, John Townsend (Raintree, 2004).

Websites

www.bbc.co.uk/science – includes information on the hunt for life on other planets and human space exploration

www.seti.org – official website of the search for Extraterrestrial Intelligence

INDEX